Alice Christiana Thompson Meynell

The Poor Sisters of Nazareth

An Illustrated Record of Life at Nazareth House, Hammersmith

Alice Christiana Thompson Meynell

The Poor Sisters of Nazareth
An Illustrated Record of Life at Nazareth House, Hammersmith

ISBN/EAN: 9783337248741

Printed in Europe, USA, Canada, Australia, Japan

Cover: Foto ©ninafisch / pixelio.de

More available books at **www.hansebooks.com**

THE ANGELUS

THE

Poor Sisters of Nazareth.

An Illustrated Record

of

Life at Nazareth House, Hammersmith

DRAWN BY

GEORGE LAMBERT;

WRITTEN BY

ALICE MEYNELL;

PUBLISHED BY

BURNS & OATES, Limited.

LONDON: 28 ORCHARD STREET, W., and 63 PATERNOSTER ROW, E.C.

AND AT NEW YORK.

TO

MY LITTLE DAUGHTER,

Monica.

PALACE COURT, LONDON, W.
1889.

The Poor Sisters of Nazareth.

NAZARETH HOUSE, with all the sanctity, shows nothing of the mystery, of the cloister. Reticence there must be, reserve, and silence as to the spiritual experience of these consecrated Sisters, but it is never made apparent. The note of the place is simply—simplicity; divine quality, which not every child possesses, and the lack of which makes middle life in the world chiefly an uncharming passage from the probable simplicity of childhood to the possible simplicity of old age and the certain simplicity of death. That Nuns are simple is one of their ways of making amends for the pranks of the world. And these Nuns are the simplest of the simple— in their dealings with their poor, with the "extern," and even with the press! If the newspaper can indirectly help them to feed their flock, the newspaper may publish their necessities and describe their enterprises; and their personal love of complete seclusion is sacrificed for the sake of charity as sweetly and undemonstratively as every other wish or thought that is touched with self.

Every one who goes to Nazareth House, therefore, is met with a welcome. The pilgrimage thither leads us past the plate-glass face and Georgian background of Kensington to the

The Choir.

beginnings of one of the shabbiest of those supplementary towns that straggle around London. If Hammersmith has nothing else to recommend it, it is certainly a good recruiting ground for Nazareth House. Misery must needs lurk in the nooks and corners of the place, for its comparative prosperities are significant of difficult living and a disheartened postponement of pauperism. The placarded groceries, the fruit languid and damp, and the dusky doubtful meat— for the acquisition of this the serried population goes daily to its work, when work is happily to be had. But all this shabby Hammersmith is further out of town, towards the river. About Nazareth House there is no squalor, but open space, with free horizon and fresh air. The large feverishly red buildings of St. Paul's School are close by, and the little Nazareth girls can watch

The Acolyte.

THE NOVICES' ORATORY.

the cricket in the field at the back and wish they were boys. The nearest houses are characteristic, ivy-grown and Georgian, with gardens. Away back to the south, fragmentary London wanders off into the sunny light, which its roofs are too distant to intercept. The garden of Nazareth House itself lies that way, and close about the house are clusters of trees with pleasant paths and resting-places in the shade. The extent of the buildings is increasing greatly. The great new wing, from the designs of Mr. Leonard Stokes, has been erected at a cost of six thousand pounds—a charge that has to be met wholly from the alms on which the Sisters feed their poor. How to find so enormous a margin when day by day it is only just possible to feed and clothe these hundreds of dependents? But the necessity was imperative. Not only were the Nuns obliged to refuse entrance to forlorn ones whom they could undertake to feed if they had the room wherein to gather them, but the inmates of the house were crowded together in a manner that hindered the liberty of the children and disturbed the silence of the dying. Nazareth House was no longer entirely the house of peace that the Nuns intended to open to the unfortunate; they could not refuse the risk of building, even though debt is the one fear of a Religious Community, and to avoid it they will deny themselves everything except their charities.

To the road the house presents the blankness of wall which is essentially conventual, and which is so rare in our many-

windowed London.   Mild red brick, slightly relieved—unlike
the school next door which flushes all over roof, walls, and
window-edges—is the material of Nazareth House.   The gate

Ironing Day.

is a type of a Gothic convent gate, with its grille and its alms-
box—things that look modern and natural in their daily use.

THE KITCHEN.

Just within, the Sister Portress has her nook, whence she appears with the grave and happy face, the only sort of face to be seen inside the pointed cap and under the sable veil of Nazareth. Her keys are not her permanent charge, for the office is held by the Sisters in turn, as is every office in this gentle Republic. Once in the enclosure, the pilgrim feels the peace that comes of sacred continuity, never to be felt in a world that does its various will and caprice morning by morning. Here is no inconstancy, no wild will, no grasping after desires and egoisms, no change except in the incidents of service and the phases of prayer, and here is none of the coming and going of thoughts that are, as we say outside, "in the air," where they produce very little, by the way, for the thought of last year

Gauffring the Cape.

will return next year, and that of this year the year after, so that if thought progresses, it does so like the planets, by turning. One of our first questions on entering the place is, What relation the life led here bears to the reviews and magazines and news-papers in which the rhythmic ebb and flow of ideas set their fugitive marks? It is almost a relief to find that the old men are allowed a paper, nay, that the Nuns are thankful to the thoughtful who send them yesterday's to beguile the leisure of palsy and weary old age. Only it is found desirable now and

c

then that a Sister should go in and allay the political passion. So the Irish Question has entered even Nazareth House; for it is not over General Boulanger or Disestablishment that the old men are tempted to shoulder their crutches.

But first of the Sisters themselves. The remarkable thing in their Order is that it combines the contemplative life and the active with a completeness, a severity, and an integrity of self-sacrifice, *ohne hast, ohne rast.*

Tea-time.

The duty of prayer is so continuous and so absorbing that it would seem to leave neither time nor strength for the duty of labour, whereas the poor and the little ones are tended with a solicitude that would exhaust ordinary women in a day. In this Order there are no lay Sisters. The whole service of the house is fulfilled by these educated ladies—the cooking, the washing and ironing, the making and mending, the per-

Preparing for Visitors.

WASHING DAY.

sonal care of the throng of children, some of them infants
in arms, their education, the nursing of the sick, the tending
of the frequent
deathbeds, and
that special work
which these Nuns
share with very
few other Com-
munities—the
Quest. And what
the Quest implies
of detailed and
minute labour
can be but va-
guely imagined
by those who
have not had to
pick over and
classify and work
at the baskets of
fragments that
remain from the
daily breaking

Two Collecting Sisters.

of bread in the great consumption of London at its dinner.
Everything here is made of scraps, and yet nothing is made of

refuse.   The most delicate care is used in the cookery, and is
even mentioned in the solemn language of the rules as a fore-
most duty of this religious life.

The Order was founded by Cardinal Wiseman, and is there-

A Collecting Van.

fore very young in the history of Catholic charity, if it is
considered in its more special character.   In a sense more
general it is as old as any other Brotherhood or Sisterhood of
the great Augustinian family, for it takes its religious Rule

from the pen of St. Augustine, and its details only from the Cardinal who sent his ecclesiastical legions "out at the Flaminian gate." Among these details is the dress, which has a character of its own, and which is said to have given the Cardinal matter for considerable study. A Religious dress should

Nazareth House, Southend.

obviously be not only grave and modest, but adapted to hard work of various kinds, when it is worn by women who do all that is done by the Nuns of Nazareth House. And it is one of the graces of the house that while some women in the world are asking, with all the energy of intending acrobats, for emancipation from their draperies, these Sisters contrive to do everything, and to do it well, muffled in close caps and hanging veils, checked by starch and enveloped in folds, and yet to keep the health and strength that make their hard life possible. It may still be permitted to wonder whether even a Cardinal would not find the burdens of his fatigues increased if his head were encased in tight *empesé* linen, and his brows so bound as to prevent that relief of grasping his overworked forehead which the most ascetic of mankind permits himself. Constraint, doubtless, becomes a second nature in a Nun; but it is curious to find how lightly it is borne, and how the delicate feminine frame fares without ever "lying down," or resting a headache upon a cushion. Doubtless the immunity of Nuns from all the inconveniences of vanity helps them to bear those of their quasi-Oriental disguise and concealment. Nevertheless an audacious fancy may sketch for itself a future when a Pope at Chicago may legislate for Sisterhoods living under the ancient interior laws, but in the midst of new and Western exterior conditions, set free from much that must be a waste of strength. The cumbrous garments of Religious Women, as they wear them now, produce a stillness of manner, especially in public, which is very distinctive. A member of a begging Order told us how once, when she was on her quest in a draper's shop—her companion being occupied with the business and she waiting alone—a hurried shopman approaching from behind took her for a dress-stand, and turned her round by the shoulders, to his own acute surprise. But with all this traditional quietness and dignity there is never a look or tone that suggests affectation or a consciousness of being better than the world.

Nuns, Novices, and Postulants form the hierarchy of the House, which is governed by the local Superior, and also —this being the Mother-house of the Order—by the Mother - General. On this lady rests

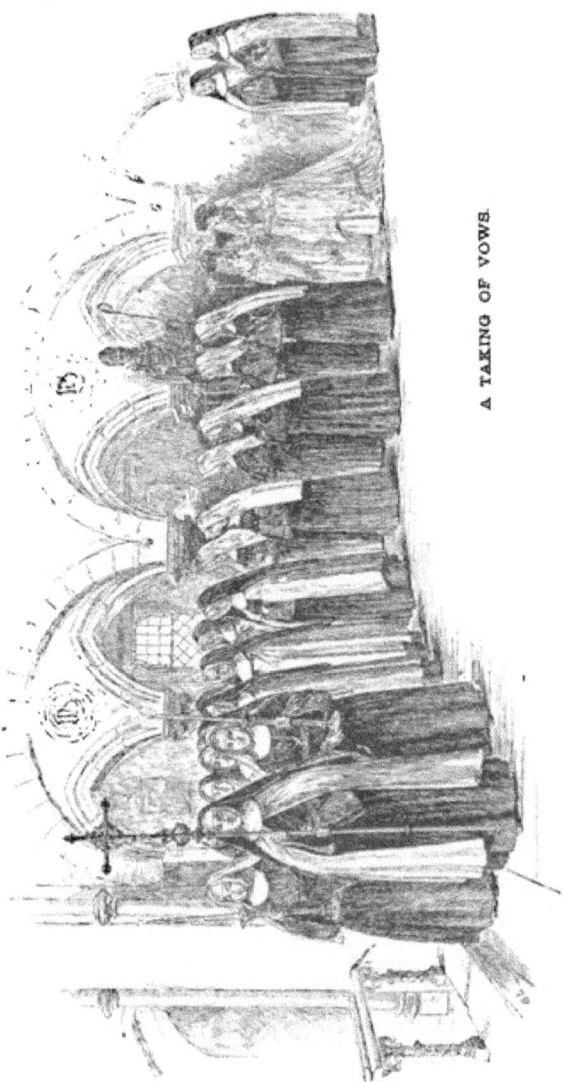

A TAKING OF VOWS.

Five o'Clock in the Morning.

the responsibility of the houses in England, Scotland, and the Colonies, the Order being an English one, and having its Apostolate to the subjects of England, white and black. The "Taking of Vows," which is one of the artist's drawings, shows the scene which appeals most strongly to the interest of outsiders. There is an obvious poetry in the bridal costume of the young creatures who have passed through the necessary severities of the Novitiate, and who are to be clad for ever after in the dress that denotes their death to the world. "There is no poetry in our after life here," says the Mother-General; "it is hard, practical work, and we pray that Heaven may send us none but Novices with sound common sense." The speaker of the phrase evidently restricted the word poetry to its rather banal allusions; the Nazareth Nuns lead, if any human beings have ever led, George Eliot's "epic life." But it is another class of poetry that is illustrated by the ceremonies of the "clothing." And the

Sisters, whose sympathy with beauty is one of their most lovable characteristics, enjoy its whole charm. It is with womanly pleasure that they describe the pretty looks of some one among them at her profession, and the care with which they curled her locks.

Nursing the Sick.

The rules of the Novitiate are the result of the experience of monasticism in its long life; and who shall say that their severity is a harder preparation than is necessary for the dying life which the Nun must lead? To the outsider the isolation of the Novices is very striking. They form together a little school under the care of the Nun who is appointed Novice-mistress, and with the other Sisters they hold no communication of companionship or speech. Nor do they take any part in the tending of the sick or in the other special duties for which the Order was formed. Their whole life is one of interior discipline and spiritual education. Even at its close, when the work of self-command and self-devotion seems so complete that the high perfection of the Religious life is to be entered upon, there is still time for further proof. The vows are taken by the Nun first for three years, then for a further three years, and not until their completion, for perpetuity. It is a little sad to hear that the Novitiate is by no means so full now as it has been. The depression of the times has affected even the supply of candidates for Religion; for a dowry is obviously indispensable for women who debar themselves from

A Sketch in the Dispensary.

ever earning a shilling for their own use, and who support their poor by begging. In certain unusual conditions the dowry may be dispensed with, but it is evident that this cannot be done unless the times are unusually good and the alms-boxes overflowing.

The days and nights of Nuns and Novices are ordered with a regularity hardly attained even by the most severe rules out-

THE DISPENSARY.

side of Religion. In prisons perhaps men live as regularly. But compare any other kind of regularity with that of this Convent. The factory is hard enough, but the "hand" himself has holidays—has some and steals others — in mitigation of a rule the yoke of which is further lightened by a kind of revenge of occasional self - indulgence. And then the peasant, who leads one of the hardest lives endured in the modern world, has at least the inevitable va-riety of nature, and the cyclic changes of the seasons, with the events of seed-time and harvest. Life in a convent has none of these. Or,

An Infirmary.

rather, they are matter of daily monotony. It is seed-time

every morning, for the perpetual renewal of the resolution that
is to effect so much; harvest every night.   The year does not
vary, except that the winter increases
the misery which is the daily sight
before the Sisters' eyes.

The qualities developed by the
active Orders of Nuns are those for
which women have gained least credit
in secular affairs—the abilities, moral
and mental, that make for organisa-
tion and discipline on a large scale.

An Aged Patient.

The "criticism of life" which is supplied by literature has long
ago and repeatedly asserted that woman is capable of subjec-
tion, and of administering and receiving
orders, when it is a question of the special
and personal relations of the family; but
that the generalities, the abstractions,
which are conditions of work on a large
scale, are fatal to its undertaking or suc-
cessful accomplishment by women. At
most it is conceded that, kept in discipline
by the strong influence of affectionate
reverence, women would work in a body

Blind Grannie.

immediately under the personal direction of a clerical head—
direction which each member should enjoy in its separate appli-

cation to herself. But even so, the world thinks, in its ready-made way of thinking, that there will continually be in such a body all the friction which comes of personal feeling. And

The Children's Infirmary.

this is the rather vulgar belief of both men and women. But meanwhile, without show or clatter or *fanfaronnade* of any kind, Religious Women have been submitting, in large bodies, to rules far more general and inexorable than any dreamed of in the

E

world's affairs; have been resigning all of their individuality which could not be brought under strict rule; have been obeying a woman, in union with women; have been organising with a mathematical attention to proportion; have been commanding with moderation, following with unanimity, doing large mono-

The Babies' Rosary.

tonous work with the precision of machinery.

And all this is done in the difficult cause of charity — of that charity which is so attractive when glanced at from without, so full of disappointments and disillusions within. But it is done in the Divine strength that cannot tire, by women whose ideal is in

Heaven, and who therefore do not take to heart the short-comings of earth, and who mingle the practices of the cloister and the choir with those of the ward and the nursery. Assuredly it is no slight power of head and hand that keeps such a charity as Nazareth House in its state of daily life and vigour. Nothing could suffice to such a work except an absolute precision in little

PATTIE.
Front view.

PATTIE.
Back view.

"Turn on, Sister!"

THE BABIES' BED-TIME.

things and an undaunted courage in great ones. The finances of the many houses are at times so low that the Mother-General confesses she has not dared to count the money in her drawer for fear of knowing for certain how little it was. And as to detail, it is only necessary to go through the house, to see the dinner preparing at the huge kitchener, and to watch the making of bed-quilts in the sewing-rooms, to understand how minutely the commonwealth of this great almshouse and con-vent is built up—or rather organised, for it is full of life in all parts.

The day begins at five o'clock for all. Though the Naza-reth Nuns do not break their night by prayer, as do the Nuns in Orders having no active work, yet theirs are neverthe-less "obedient slumbers." For one Sister, at least, in every twenty-four hours the day never ends at all, each one taking in rotation her turn for watching the wards at night, a duty which excuses her from nothing of the routine of the following day's labours or prayers. At five the Nuns, who rise from straw mattresses, gather in the chapel, where half-an-hour's meditation follows the morning prayer and precedes Mass. After Mass comes the Office, with other prayers, and thanksgiving, and not till then do the Sisters take their breakfast of bread and butter. At all their meals they fare like their poor, their food being principally the broken food of alms; and so severe are they in their abstinence from luxuries, that if game is sent to them as a present they touch none of it themselves. They dine, moreover, at an uncovered table. It appears from the rules that prayers and the duties of devotion are always postponed, if necessary, to the duties of charity, but though postponed are never dispensed with. Nevertheless there is nowhere a face that confesses fatigue. Charity here never loses its bloom of gaiety. It would be a sad house indeed if the Nuns were not gay.

For that is a helpless crowd for which the Sisters of Nazareth are working, building, and praying. The very presence of the active and helpful Nuns seems to set forth more clearly the forlorn weakness of these children, old and young. Here the oldest of ancient women, whose face is extinguished and null with the shadow of coming death, lies silent and serene in the cheerful ward; here the orphaned baby lies in the virginal arms of the Nun, more tender than many a mother's; there the incurable child rests, on some pretty patchwork cushion, the little head that will never meet the storms of the world; there, again, is the poor girl born with some affliction that will for ever prevent her from leaving the walls which gave her hapless infancy a refuge; there, again, is the blind imbecile, proud of the one thing she can do— the singing of little songs—and delighted with the kind applause of the Sisters; yonder is "the oldest man that ever wore grey hairs," taking a little comfort from his pipe and from his newspaper, watching with his dim eyes the activity of the mere septuagenarian who is strong enough to chop the wood and

THE CLASS ROOM.

fetch and carry for the house.   And all this little population—
more than poor, more than forlorn—is dependent upon the fore-
sight, the skill, the vigilance, the constant tenderness of the
Sisters of Nazareth.   All these meals, all these garments, and
many a little indulgence which sick infancy and extreme old age
can scarcely live without, are gathered by the Nuns—humble
labourers, voluntary mendicants, who follow gleaning in the
wake of the pageant of luxury and wealth which goes "to and
fro in the world, and up and down in it."

The forlorn women taken into the refuge are always called
"the old ladies."   It is one of the customs of the house.   If
there is one among them who has a face beautiful in form or
expression, the Nuns do not fail to draw their visitors' attention
to it; and some of these faces are in fact most beautiful and
spiritual.   Even those who are suffering are peaceful; those
who are passing into eternity without pain look like old saints,
pale not with the difficulty of common life and poverty, but with
seventy years of prayers.   Some other old ladies, who are dressed
and grouped.at work and talk in the long sitting-rooms, have
a cheerfulness much more of this world.   They have jokes on
one another's little failings, much enjoyed by the subjects.   To
a very few, old age has restored a gaiety more pathetic; they
have childish impulses, all in the direction of jollity.   One
expresses her satisfaction with the disposition of the world by
which she has been landed in an almshouse, a pauper after a

F

life of labour, by improvising a dance.   Another, "Grannie," who
is blind and a great pet, sits in her perpetual darkness waiting
only for the step of one of the Nuns, her special love.   "Is

The Work-room.

it Sister Mary?" she asks, clinging to the hand of her dear
protectress, who touches her on her way round the rooms; she
also is happy, though in what conditions, as the world would

judge them! She pretends to scold her Nun for a long absence, and one imagines the playful little scene to be enacted day by day, with the sweet-humoured persistence of the aged, who never tire. Another noticeable figure is that of a graceful old Frenchwoman, whose white hair, very carefully dressed, suggests a coiffure of the last century, and who speaks with an educated accent. Here and there in the women's wards are bird-cages, for there are crumbs left over from even the table of the poor; and no doubt it is a welcome variation of experience for those who are dependent upon others for the necessities of every day to have a linnet or a canary dependent upon them. The hands of most are busily employed, and in no distasteful work. The patching of minute pieces of silk and satin in geometrical designs—and the whole house is, as it were, draped in shreds and patches—gives them an interest that seems never to flag. The Sisters, in passing, praise the taste of this one in colour, and of that one in design; and altogether nothing could be more unlike a *corvée*. These workers are, of course, the younger of the aged; among the elder there are too many hands crippled and deformed with the general affliction—rheumatism. These show their sorrows to the visitor with a certain sense of distinction probably not without its consolation. In this house the sufferer is considered to be favoured by God, and there is no shame. But among such a motley gathering of generally undisciplined tempers and minds more or less irresponsible, is there no grumbling, is there neither

jealousy nor friction, neither the common fastidiousness of the
destitute nor the ingratitude of the helpless? Who has ever
known an almshouse or a hospital without these? They may

The Soup-Kitchen.

exist at Nazareth House, but if so they are invisible, and it is
easier to believe in a minor miracle of sweet temper.

Moreover, in the children's wards there is something like a
miracle of perpetual merriment. No nursery, appointed with

all that can be devised or bought, can show such peace and pleasure. Ailing young babies sit up, propped in their cots, and look on with their pale faces at the games of the children, perfectly content. There seems to be no quarrelling. On one visit only did we hear a single cry—the most unwonted of sounds in this poor orphanage. There had been a tumble. One round child had rolled over another. A Sister ran to the rescue, and the cry was hushed. The mob of little ones troop to the door to greet us, and their joyful noise had gone out to meet us a long way down the corridor. They pause in their playing and dancing down the long gay room, and run forward with a confidence that has an infinite significance. Children that do so have never been snubbed or discouraged or suppressed, or oppressed by the sadness of minds less innocent than theirs. Who, in the world, has not had remorse for inflicting this oppression, if no other? Here simplicity is nursed and taught by simplicity. And the less sweet ways of discipline which less wise women can hardly do without, if they have a brood of four or five to keep in partial subordination, seem to be quite unnecessary here, where a hundred or two have to be kept in the absolute order without which such a mob would fall into a state of infantile anarchy and nihilism. And the listlessness common to luxurious children outside, and the other kind of apathy which belongs to the poor, are unknown here. There is not a look to show *ennui* or restlessness or discontent. The little ones are full of interest. About a lady visitor they will cluster eagerly, to look at her ornaments, to open her parasol, and gather in a group of sweet faces under its shadow; to clasp her knees and win her to a romp with them on the floor. Each child is carefully dressed—not only in clean garments, but in pretty ones. There is no frock that is not gracefully made and gaily trimmed. The infinite variety of the odds and ends has a charming effect as regards the children, whose colouring has been studiously suited, and who have that look of having been separately and individually cared for which takes something from the melancholy of the sight of an orphan crowd. The White Lady who rose nightly from her grave, in the German legend, to wash and comb her little children, ill tended after her death, need not walk the wards of Nazareth House. The dead-and-gone mothers whose little ones are there can rest in peace.

From the Incurable Children's Ward the sounds are stiller. In several cases there is an eternal silence, for not a few are dumb; but more are blind. One poor girl is shut away from all messages from her kind, except the message which comes through the Sister's caressing hand on her shoulder. Another was rescued from some dark hole in which her deformed and blighted face had been hidden away. Another, born without arms—a sweet-faced rosy girl—will never be able to labour in the world to which her young health and spirits would lead her;

the Sisters have taught her to write with her mouth. Another young girl is afflicted with some disease of the nerves, which keeps her head and hands in perpetual movement. Yet an-

The Summer-House.

other—a girl of full age—sits nursing a doll, which she cunningly hides away at any approach, for fear this treasure should be taken from her. These afflictions soften away in the atmosphere of Nazareth House. An incurable child, once received, need never leave. If her incurable life is long, she grows up and passes into old age and dies there.

Besides this infirmary, there is another important department—the school in which girls are educated in lofty rooms and pure air, and in the moral atmosphere of order, duty, and busy kindness, for life in domestic service. After the usual education, they are taught to make themselves useful in the many offices of Nazareth House, and at sixteen or seventeen they are placed as servants. "We never lose sight of one of them," says the Mother-General; "we keep up a correspondence with them, and when they have holidays they come and see us." In times of illness during their subsequent lives, too, the Nazareth girls are received again and nursed back to health.

As with the old people, so with the children, there is no religious test whatever for admission into Nazareth House. The wishes of parents—when there are parents and when they have wishes—are carefully respected. But children are not kept within the Home after the age of First Communion unless they are Catholics, or unless their parents are willing that they should become such. The Nuns find that it is not possible for them to take the responsibilities of consciences more than twelve or fourteen years old, and unguided by the rules of definite religious order. The difficulty is intelligible. With the old people, who have none outside in the world to decide for them, the

religious test is not applied at all. On Sundays they go at will
to their various chapels, and their death is tended by their own
ministers. But this charity is doubtless better known and more
attractive to the Catholic poor than to the rest.

The separation of the very old people from the very young
ones has made Nazareth House a complete home. The noise

Veterans.

which breaks out of the nursery and
the schoolroom alike convinces us of
the necessity. Extreme old age has slumbers which are light
and short and few; it watches with wide-open eyes the flicker-
ing of a lamp through a long night, and if the wished-for
sleep comes "when day is blue in the window-blind," it is hard
to have it broken. And besides, when you come to ninety
years, you like nothing louder than the tender voice of the
Sister in your ward; and the dying love silence. Nor was

G

additional space needed for the children only. The old men and women overflowed the rooms in which they were first gathered. Old people live so long under tender care that those who come knocking at the door for admittance are more numerous than those who pass away to the only refuge which is still quieter. At Nazareth House there is none of the voluntary or the involuntary unkindness; there is none of the inevitable impatience that in the homes of misery outside shortens disease, and hurries old age, and "speeds the parting guest;" here the dying are in no haste to die.

In addition to the internal work of the house, the Sisters have undertaken during the last few winters a soup-kitchen, which has brought several hundred starving people from all parts of London daily to their gates. The Sisters have risen to set on their cauldrons at half-past four on the winter mornings. And it has been hard to find the wherewithal. Sometimes the inmates have voluntarily given up their share, the food which is inevitably an important incident of their days, to the outsiders —men cowering in the hard frost, and in some cases literally fainting from famine. One thousand nine hundred persons, all told, have eaten their bread in one day in Nazareth House, until the last of all the fragments has been consumed. The soup-kitchen is absolutely free. The Sisters found that in the conditions of the unemployed it was best to put no obstacle, not even that of a ticket, in the way of approach to this daily food.

MIDWINTER.

DISTRIBUTION OF SOUP.

No questions are asked of man, woman, or child. Only it was found necessary to keep the charity for the unemployed by giving the soup a little before noon. Men at work were tempted to take advantage of a twelve o'clock dole. As it is, the great number of men and the comparative fewness of the women and children are noticeable, and imply long journeys to Hammersmith. On the intensely frosty mornings of midwinter ragged men are to be seen tramping westwards from distances whither it might have been thought that the fame of Nazareth had never penetrated. They straggle out by twos and threes, starting early, and waiting before the door with its cross. Within, they get their hot portions—an excellent *olla podrida*—in the shed, and eat it on benches grouped at the feet of the great crucifix. It is impossible, looking at these men, silent and uncommunicative and unobservant in their misery, tired with the long tramp that must be heavy payment for a meal, to question the rightness of the Sisters' work of relief. Whatever a riper justice than that of our own time may decide as to the general debt owed by the nation to its poor, the payment of this little matter of

The Daily Dole at the Gate.

interest cannot compromise the larger question. It is the immediate and fugitive succour of want so urgent that no reply is possible except that of the gift in an outstretched hand.

To have been as a casual visitor for an hour in this refuge is to take away an alms not explicitly intended by the Order. For to live in a great city is to live surrounded by horrible evils—frenzied self-indulgences, cruelties, pangs in the hearts of the helpless, the acquiescence of children to despair, religious egoism, and other things that "make a goblin of the sun." And there often arises the foolish wish to breathe air not so burdened and darkened. But we leave Nazareth House convinced that to live in a great city is also to live surrounded by unsleeping pity—nowhere more vigilant or more effectual than in the places where, gathering the unfortunate to their hearts,

> "The Brides of Christ
> Lie hid, emparadised."

The Branch Houses of THE POOR SISTERS OF NAZARETH *are at—*

Aberdeen, N.B.

Cardiff, South Wales.

Southend, Essex.

Oxford.

Northampton.

Lenton, Nottingham.

Ballynafeigh, Belfast.

Middlesbrough.

Southsea.

Cheltenham.

Cape Town, South Africa.

Kimberley, South Africa.

Port Elizabeth, South Africa.

Ballarat, Australia.

www.ingramcontent.com/pod-product-compliance
Lightning Source LLC
Chambersburg PA
CBHW022042080426
42733CB00007B/938